LET'S
TALK

My brother is
autistic

Written by Jennifer Moore-Mallinos

Illustrated by Marta Fàbrega

SALARIYA
BH
BOOK HOUSE

4

This book
belongs to:

....

....

Do you have any brothers or sisters?
I do! I have one brother; his name is Billy and
he has autism. Billy and I have a lot of fun
together. Most of the time we get along, but I
don't like it when he freaks out, especially in
front of my friends or the other children
at school.

Like lunchtime yesterday in the school cafeteria. We were together, and Billy had just lined up his biscuits, the way he always does before he eats them. One of the other kids asked Billy if he could have a biscuit. Billy ignored him and kept admiring his row of biscuits, so the boy asked again. Billy just repeated the question. The boy thought Billy was making fun of him, so he grabbed one of the biscuits. And that's when it happened...

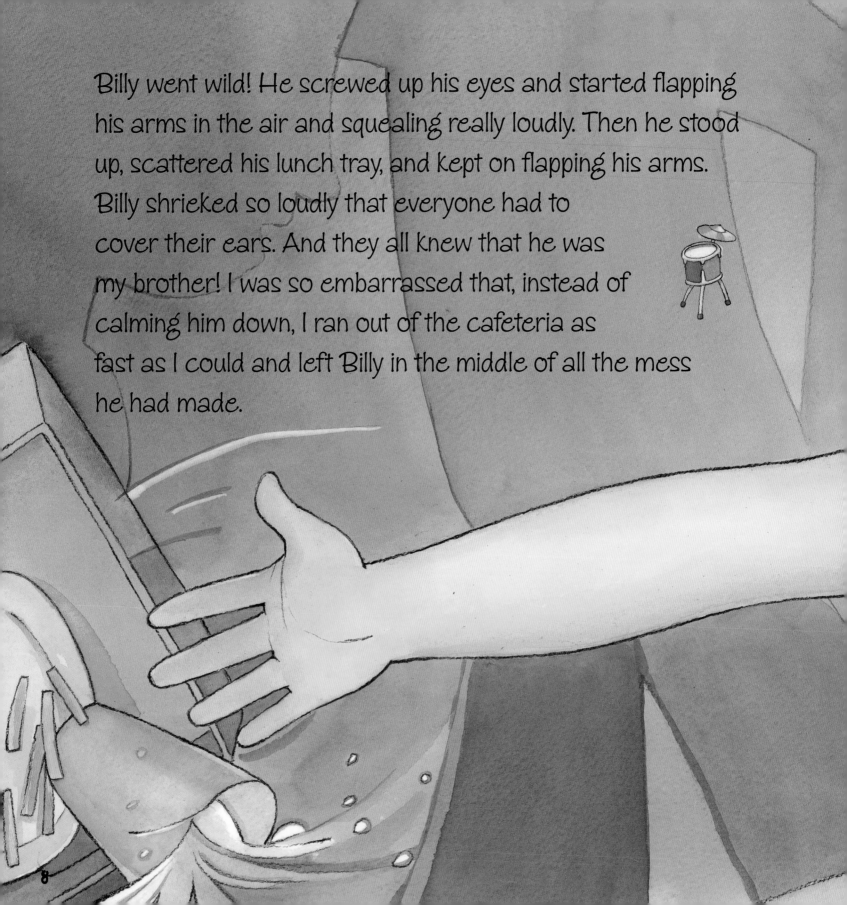

Billy went wild! He screwed up his eyes and started flapping his arms in the air and squealing really loudly. Then he stood up, scattered his lunch tray, and kept on flapping his arms. Billy shrieked so loudly that everyone had to cover their ears. And they all knew that he was my brother! I was so embarrassed that, instead of calming him down, I ran out of the cafeteria as fast as I could and left Billy in the middle of all the mess he had made.

9

I kept running until I ran straight into Mrs Smitty, my teacher. I told her what had happened and how everybody, especially the kids in my class, were staring and pointing at Billy, and how some were even laughing at him!

I knew that the boy wasn't trying to be mean by taking the biscuit; he just didn't understand Billy. Billy always likes things to be the same, like the way he lines up his biscuits in a row before he eats them. If things change too quickly, Billy gets confused. Flapping his arms or rocking back and forward again and again helps him to feel better.

Maybe if he knew more about autism the boy wouldn't have taken one of Billy's biscuits. He would have known how important it is not to change the way Billy does things. I told my teacher that I wished the kids understood autism more, because if they did, then maybe they'd be more patient with Billy.

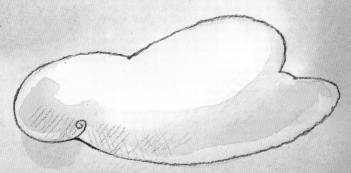

Mrs Smitty told me that scientists are trying to find out what causes autism, but nobody knows for sure yet. Autism may run in families, but some people believe that children with autism have special allergies and sensitivities that make them think and behave differently. An autistic brain works differently from other people's brains. Autism can't be cured, and that's why everybody has to learn about it. Mrs Smitty said that making fun of Billy was unkind, and that we must help the other children to understand. She said that she had an idea, and hurried off to her classroom.

The bell rang and it was time to go
back to class. I was a bit scared
about seeing the other kids in case
they started making jokes
about Billy again. But when
I walked into my classroom,
Mrs Smitty and some of
the other kids were busy taping a
whole bunch of pictures to the board,
so nobody noticed me as I came in
and sat down.

The pictures were of different people, young and old. They were all doing different things: there was a young man playing the piano, a girl playing tennis and even a picture of an old man painting a portrait of a beautiful lady. The picture I liked best was of a boy called Jason McElwain, who made the winning basket for our basketball team. He looked so happy! All of these people loved what they were doing and were so good at it that some of them were even famous.

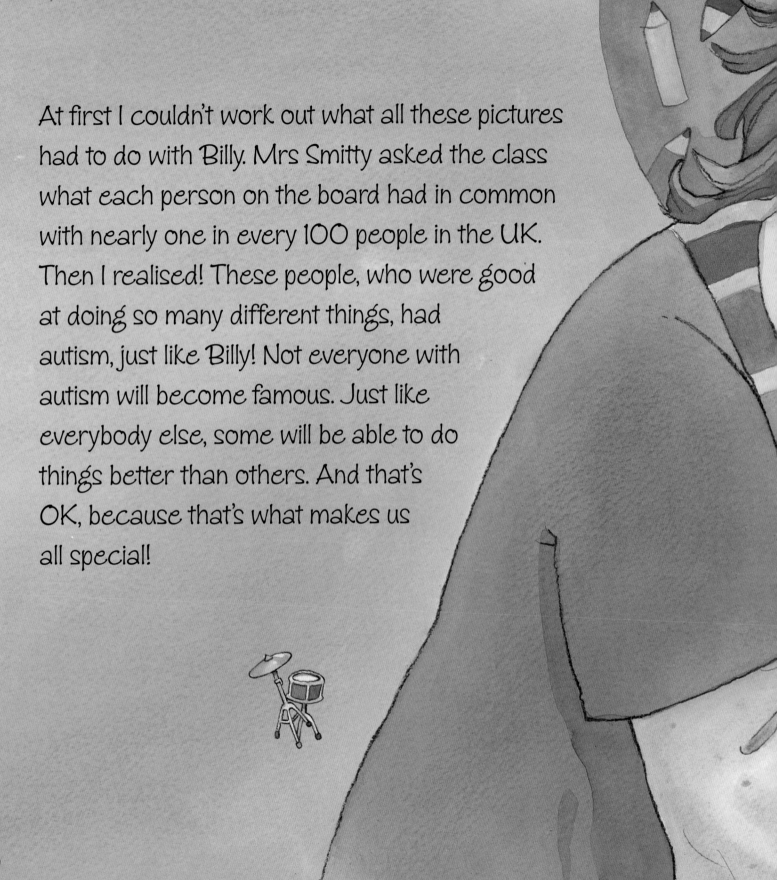

At first I couldn't work out what all these pictures had to do with Billy. Mrs Smitty asked the class what each person on the board had in common with nearly one in every 100 people in the UK. Then I realised! These people, who were good at doing so many different things, had autism, just like Billy! Not everyone with autism will become famous. Just like everybody else, some will be able to do things better than others. And that's OK, because that's what makes us all special!

Wow! It was hard to believe, but it was true: Even though all these people had autism, they had all found something that they could do really well. Billy's really good at playing the drums, so maybe when he grows up he'll play in a band and, being his brother, he'll give me front-row tickets to watch him play! Now, that would be cool!

Mrs Smitty talked a lot about what it was like to have autism. She said that autistic kids sometimes have trouble doing what their teacher or parents ask them to do, or can get frustrated and upset really quickly when something changes — like Billy's row of biscuits. Most kids with autism like to do things alone and, because they find it hard to start a conversation with others, it's not always easy for them to make friends. Others have trouble learning things like reading and writing and maths. Billy needs some extra help, so he has a special teacher who stays with him in class and helps him if he needs it. She is very patient and knows how to keep him calm.

When class was over and the other kids
had left, I thanked Mrs Smitty for what
she had done. She had made it clear
that Billy had the right to be himself, a child with
autism, and she had also made it OK for me to
be his brother without feeling embarrassed.
I'll never leave Billy alone again. And next time
Billy gets cross or starts talking to himself,
I hope the other kids will remember that Billy is
autistic and that's OK!

 On the way home with Billy, I realised that not only had I seen who he is, but who he could become. I told Billy that I was sorry for leaving him all alone in the cafeteria and I promised that no matter what, I would never do that again. Billy smiled, touched my shoulder and said 'You're IT!' and then ran away. As always, I counted to ten before I started chasing him and, as always, Billy ran as fast as he could all the way home!

Note to Parents

The purpose of this book is to acknowledge the prevalence of autism among children and to recognise some of the realities children with autism and their families – in particular their siblings – may experience. This book gives us the opportunity to consider some of the challenges a sibling of an autistic child may experience on a regular basis.

It is hoped that this book will promote a better understanding and acceptance of children who have been diagnosed with autism, and also of the difficulties their siblings must face.

Did you know that, according to the National Autistic Society in the UK, nearly one person in 100 has an autistic-spectrum disorder (including Asperger syndrome)? And many of these children with autism have brothers and sisters.

Siblings of children with autism often share common concerns and similar sources of stress. These may include a fear of teasing and ridicule among their peers, or feelings of embarrassment, frustration and even anger towards the child's autistic behaviour. Children may also feel some level of resentment towards their parents and/or teachers, believing that they are not receiving the same amount of attention as their sibling with autism and therefore are not being treated fairly.

Autism is considered a spectrum disorder characterised by a set of behaviours exhibited along a continuum, ranging from mild to quite severe. Although an individual may display a combination of behavioural traits that fall within a specific range from mild to severe, autism is unique to one's personality.

The National Autistic Society advises that: 'Early diagnosis and the right education and support can all help people with autism to fulfil their potential.'

Behaviour that is characteristic of autism is usually first detected through the parents' observation of their child's everyday behaviour, including the ability to communicate and socialise with others. Distinctive autistic traits may not become apparent until the early childhood years, between the ages of 2 and 6.

According to the National Autistic Society, children with autism usually:

- find it hard to understand non-verbal communication, such as facial expressions and tone of voice
- take language very literally and find metaphors and idioms confusing and sometimes frightening
- have difficulty recognising people's feelings or expressing their own, so they find it hard to understand social conventions such as the give-and-take nature of conversations
- struggle to understand and predict people's behaviour, and find change and unexpected situations stressful
- have a strong preference for routines and can develop intense, sometimes 'obsessive', special interests
- don't engage in imaginary play, preferring to act out something they've seen and repeating the same scene over and over again.

Many children with autism are over- or under-sensitive to certain sounds, light, touch, smells and tastes, and they may avoid or seek out sensory stimuli.*

Although siblings of autistic children seem to cope well overall, there are some things that parents can do to help to make family life run more smoothly:

- It is always a good idea to give siblings the information they need to understand autism. The information you provide for your child should take into account their age and level of understanding. Explaining autism to children should start early and be done often. As your children mature, so will the information you provide to increase their level of understanding of autism.
- Some children may have a difficult time forming a relationship with their autistic sibling. Attempts to engage their sibling will not always be successful, and can leave them feeling rejected and discouraged from trying again. Parents can help their children to build friendship with one another by teaching simple skills that will help to engage the autistic child. For example, make sure that the autistic sibling is paying attention, give simple instructions, and give ongoing praise during play.
- Provide one-to-one time with the other children in the family. Make it clear that they are special, too. All children want to feel special and to feel that things around them are fair or equal, particularly at home.

Growing up in a family with a child who has autism can be difficult at times, but most family members seem to cope well. And although siblings will learn to deal with specific issues sooner in life than others, they will discover that the love, patience and sense of humour they have learned are vital life skills that they can use for the rest of their lives.

*Extracts from *After diagnosis: Information for parents and carers of children with autism* reproduced with permission. Copyright The National Autistic Society 2012. www.autism.org.uk.

Other titles in this series:
My friend has Down's syndrome
The colours of the rainbow
Daddy's getting married
When my parents forgot
how to be friends
I remember
Lost and found
Have you got a secret?

Visit our **new** online shop at
shop.salariya.com
for great offers, gift ideas,
all our new releases and
free postage and packaging.

Published in Great Britain in MMXIII by
Book House, an imprint of
The Salariya Book Company Ltd
25 Marlborough Place, Brighton BN1 1UB
www.salariya.com
www.book-house.co.uk

1 3 5 7 9 8 6 4 2

A CIP catalogue record for this book is available
from the British Library.

Printed and bound in China.

PB ISBN: 978-1-908973-24-5

Original title of the book in Spanish: Mi hermano es autista
© Copyright MMVIII by Gemser Publications, S.L.
El Castell, 38; Teià (08329) Barcelona, Spain (World Rights)